Psychology in Practice:

Strategies for Success

By Steven Orchard

theBizpreneurs Publishing, 2023

Index:

Chapter 1: Introduction to Business Psychology, *3*

Chapter 2: Positive Psychology in Business, *11*

Chapter 3: Cognitive Psychology in Marketing and Consumer Behavior., *21*

Chapter 4: Operant Conditioning in Human Resource, *32*

Chapter 5: Social Psychology in Business, *41*

Chapter 6: Developmental Psychology and its Application in Human Resource Practices, *51*

Chapter 7: Abnormal Psychology in the Workplace., *62*

Chapter 8: Biological Psychology and its Implications for Operations and Marketing., *72*

Chapter 9: Psychodynamic Theory in Human Resources and Leadership, *83*

Chapter 10: Positive Psychology in Business., *90*

Chapter 1: Introduction to Business Psychology

Businesses are complex ecosystems where human psychology plays a central role in shaping outcomes. Understanding the principles of psychology and their application in the business world is fundamental for success in today's highly competitive and dynamic environments. This book aims to explore the intersection of psychology and business, providing insights into how psychological concepts can be harnessed to enhance customer relations, consumer behaviors, marketing strategies, networking, partnerships, human resources practices, and operations.

In this introductory chapter, we will set the stage for the exploration of these topics by highlighting the significance of psychology in the business landscape. We will also outline the structure and objectives of this book, emphasizing its practical relevance for professionals and business students. Additionally, we will provide a brief overview of the major psychology topics that will be discussed in subsequent chapters and their relevance to various aspects of business.

The Significance of Psychology in Business

Psychology is the scientific study of human behavior and mental processes. In the context of business, psychology serves as a powerful lens through which we can better understand the motivations, preferences, and decision-making processes of individuals and groups.

This understanding, in turn, can be leveraged to achieve a wide range of business objectives.

Customer Relations and Consumer Behavior

One of the cornerstones of successful businesses is the ability to build and maintain strong customer relationships. Psychology helps us comprehend the needs, expectations, and emotions of customers. By applying principles such as social psychology, businesses can enhance their understanding of customer behavior, tailor marketing efforts, and improve customer service. For example, understanding the principles of social influence can guide businesses in creating persuasive advertising campaigns that resonate with target audiences.

Marketing Strategies

Marketing is inherently tied to psychology. Effective marketing relies on an understanding of consumer psychology, including perception, memory, motivation, and decision-making processes. Cognitive psychology informs how marketing materials are designed to capture and hold consumers' attention, while behavioral psychology principles underpin strategies to encourage desired consumer behaviors. An understanding of emotions and motivations helps craft compelling marketing messages and campaigns.

Networking and Partnerships

Networking and forming strategic partnerships are essential for business growth and success. Social psychology insights can be invaluable in this context, offering guidance on building rapport, effective communication, and negotiating mutually beneficial agreements. Moreover, cross-cultural psychology helps businesses navigate the complexities of working with partners from different cultural backgrounds.

Human Resources Practices

Human resources are at the heart of an organization's success. Psychologically informed practices can help in talent acquisition, training, employee engagement, and conflict resolution. By understanding the principles of motivation and leadership, businesses can foster a positive work environment that promotes employee well-being and productivity.

Operations

Operational efficiency is critical for any business. Insights from cognitive psychology can optimize processes by simplifying decision-making, reducing cognitive load, and improving task performance. Additionally, knowledge of the psychology of teamwork and collaboration can lead to more effective group dynamics within organizations.

<u>Objectives of this Book</u>

The primary objectives of this book are as follows:

1. Provide Practical Insights: This book aims to bridge the gap between psychological theories and practical applications in the business world. Readers will gain actionable insights into how to leverage psychological principles to achieve business goals.

2. Explore Key Psychology Topics: We will delve into essential psychology topics, including classical conditioning, operant conditioning, cognitive psychology, social psychology, developmental psychology, abnormal psychology, biological psychology, psychodynamic theory, positive

psychology, behavioral psychology, cross-cultural psychology, and the psychology of emotion and motivation.

3. Relate Psychology to Business: Each psychology topic will be explored in the context of various business principles such as customer relations, consumer behaviors, marketing, networking, partnerships, human resources, and operations. Real-world examples and case studies will illustrate the practical application of these principles.

4. Promote Critical Thinking: We encourage readers to think critically about how psychological concepts can be adapted and integrated into their specific business situations. Exercises and discussion questions at the end of each chapter will facilitate this process.

5. Provide Resources for Further Exploration: In addition to in-text citations, each chapter will include a list of recommended resources for readers who wish to explore specific topics in greater depth.

Conclusion

Psychology is an indispensable tool for businesses seeking to thrive in today's competitive and rapidly evolving landscape. This book aims to equip professionals and students with the knowledge and skills to leverage psychological principles effectively in their business endeavors. As we delve into each psychology topic and its application in business, we invite readers to embark on a journey of discovery and practical application, ultimately enhancing their ability to succeed in the world of business.

Chapter 2: Positive Psychology in Business: Enhancing Employee Satisfaction, Customer Loyalty, and Well-being

Positive psychology, a branch of psychology focused on studying human strengths, well-being, and flourishing, offers valuable insights and strategies that can be applied to various aspects of business operations. By incorporating positive psychology principles into customer relations and human resource practices, organizations can foster a positive work culture, leverage employee strengths, and promote work-life balance, ultimately leading to higher employee engagement, customer satisfaction, and overall well-being. This chapter explores the significance of positive psychology in the business context, highlighting its potential benefits and providing practical recommendations for its implementation.

Positive Psychology in Customer Relations:

Incorporating positive psychology principles in customer relations is essential for creating positive customer experiences, building customer loyalty, and generating customer satisfaction. Research has shown that positive emotions can enhance customers' perceptions of service quality and increase their likelihood of repeat purchases (Fredrickson, 2003). By focusing on positive emotions, businesses can design customer interactions that foster positive experiences, such as training customer service representatives to be empathetic, attentive, and responsive to customer needs

(Cohn & Fredrickson, 2010). Implementing positive psychology interventions in customer relations can lead to improved customer satisfaction, increased customer loyalty, and positive word-of-mouth recommendations.

Moreover, the concept of strengths-based approach, derived from positive psychology, can be applied in customer relations. Recognizing and leveraging customers' strengths, such as their unique preferences or skills, can enhance their satisfaction and engagement with a product or service. For instance, businesses can personalize their offerings based on customers' strengths and provide tailored recommendations, resulting in a more meaningful and positive customer experience (Linley, Willars, & Biswas-Diener, 2010).

Positive Psychology in Human Resource Practices:

Positive psychology principles are equally relevant in human resource practices, influencing employee satisfaction, engagement, and overall well-being. Fostering a positive work culture is crucial in creating an environment that supports and nurtures employees' psychological needs. Research suggests that a positive work culture characterized by trust, respect, and gratitude can lead to higher job satisfaction, reduced turnover, and increased employee commitment (Cameron, Bright, & Caza, 2004).

Emphasizing employee strengths is another important aspect of positive psychology in human resource practices. By recognizing and utilizing employees' strengths, organizations can enhance their job satisfaction and performance. This can be achieved by providing training and development opportunities that align with employees' strengths, assigning tasks that allow them to utilize their strengths, and offering feedback and recognition for their contributions (Luthans, Avey, Avolio, Norman, & Combs, 2006). Leveraging employee strengths not only boosts individual well-being but also contributes to overall team productivity and organizational success.

Promoting work-life balance is another critical component of positive psychology in human resource practices. Balancing work and personal life is crucial for employees' well-being, satisfaction, and productivity. Organizations can facilitate work-life balance by implementing flexible work arrangements, promoting employee autonomy and control over their work schedules, and encouraging employees to prioritize self-care and maintain healthy boundaries (Greenhaus & Powell, 2006). Such practices contribute to reduced stress levels, increased job satisfaction, and improved overall well-being.

<u>Implementation Strategies:</u>

Implementing positive psychology principles requires a systematic approach that involves integrating them into various aspects of the organization's policies, practices, and culture. Here are some practical strategies for incorporating positive psychology in customer relations and human resource practices:

1. Training and Education: Provide training programs and workshops for employees to enhance their understanding of positive psychology principles, including the importance of positive emotions, strengths-based approaches, and work-life balance.

2. Recruitment and Selection: Incorporate positive psychology principles in the recruitment and

selection process by assessing candidates' strengths, positive attitudes, and alignment with the organization's values and culture.

3. Performance Management: Develop performance management systems that focus on recognizing and reinforcing employee strengths, providing constructive feedback, and setting meaningful goals that align with employees' personal values and strengths.

4. Rewards and Recognition: Implement reward and recognition programs that acknowledge and celebrate employee achievements, emphasizing the positive impact of their contributions to the organization's success.

5. Leadership Development: Train leaders in positive leadership practices, such as fostering positive

relationships, promoting a positive work culture, and inspiring and empowering employees.

6. Employee Well-being Programs: Establish initiatives that prioritize employee well-being, such as wellness programs, stress management workshops, and work-life balance initiatives.

Conclusion:

Incorporating positive psychology principles into customer relations and human resource practices offers numerous benefits for businesses, including increased employee satisfaction, improved customer loyalty, and enhanced overall well-being. By fostering a positive work culture, leveraging employee strengths, and promoting work-life balance, organizations can create an environment that nurtures employee engagement and positively impacts customer experiences. Implementing these principles requires a

systematic and holistic approach, integrating positive

psychology strategies into various aspects of the

organization's operations. By embracing positive

psychology, businesses can create a thriving workplace

and build sustainable relationships with customers,

ultimately driving organizational success.

References:

Cameron, K. S., Bright, D., & Caza, A. (2004).

Exploring the relationships between organizational

virtuousness and performance. American Behavioral

Scientist, 47(6), 766-790.

Cohn, M. A., & Fredrickson, B. L. (2010). In search

of durable positive psychology interventions:

Predictors and consequences of long-term positive

behavior change. Journal of Positive Psychology,

5(5), 355-366.

Fredrickson, B. L. (2003). The value of positive

emotions: The emerging science of positive

psychology is coming to understand why it's good to

feel good. American Scientist, 91(4), 330-335.

Greenhaus, J. H., & Powell, G. N. (2006). When

work and family are allies: A theory of work-family

enrichment. Academy of Management Review,

31(1), 72-92.

Linley, P. A., Willars, J., & Biswas-Diener, R.

(Eds.). (2010). The strengths book: Be confident, be

successful, and enjoy better relationships by

realizing the best of you. CAPP Press.

Luthans, F., Avey, J. B., Avolio, B. J., Norman, S.

M., & Combs, G. M. (2006). Psychological capital

development: Toward a micro-intervention. Journal

of Organizational Behavior, 27(3), 387-393.

Chapter 3: Cognitive Psychology and its

Applications in Marketing and Consumer Behavior

Cognitive psychology, a branch of psychology that focuses on the study of mental processes, has significant implications for understanding how consumers perceive, process, and remember information. In the realm of business, this understanding plays a crucial role in designing effective marketing strategies, advertisements, product placements, and user interfaces that align with consumers' cognitive capabilities and preferences. This chapter explores the key concepts of cognitive psychology and demonstrates their practical applications in marketing and consumer behavior.

Perception and Consumer Behavior:

Perception is the process through which individuals interpret and make sense of sensory information from their environment. In marketing, understanding how consumers perceive stimuli such as advertisements, packaging, and branding is essential for creating a favorable impression. Research suggests that factors such as attention, sensory cues, and context significantly influence perception. For instance, marketers can leverage the principle of selective attention to design advertisements that stand out and capture consumers' attention amidst a sea of competing stimuli (Cherry, 2020). By employing attention-grabbing visuals, contrasting colors, and compelling messaging, businesses can increase the likelihood of consumers attending to their marketing materials.

Furthermore, cognitive psychology highlights the role of perception in shaping consumer preferences and judgments. The mere exposure effect suggests that individuals tend to develop a preference for stimuli they are repeatedly exposed to (Zajonc, 1968). This finding has implications for brand exposure and familiarity. Businesses can leverage this effect by strategically placing their brands and products in consumers' environments, fostering repeated exposure and increasing the likelihood of favorable consumer attitudes.

Information Processing and Decision-Making:

Cognitive psychology also sheds light on how consumers process information and make decisions.

Consumers are information processors who engage in various cognitive processes, such as attention, encoding, storage, and retrieval. Understanding these processes is crucial for designing effective marketing messages and facilitating consumer decision-making.

First, the limited capacity of attention and working memory highlights the importance of presenting information in a concise and easily digestible manner. By simplifying complex information, businesses can facilitate consumers' cognitive processing and enhance comprehension (Kahneman, 2011). This principle is particularly relevant in designing websites, mobile applications, and other user interfaces where information overload can hinder consumer engagement.

Furthermore, cognitive psychology emphasizes the significance of encoding and retrieval processes in

consumer memory. The levels-of-processing theory
suggests that the depth of information processing
influences memory recall (Craik & Lockhart, 1972). By
creating meaningful and personally relevant
associations with their products or services, businesses
can enhance the likelihood of consumers encoding and
retrieving positive brand information.

Memory and Branding:

Memory plays a vital role in consumer behavior,
as it influences brand awareness, brand recognition, and
brand recall. Cognitive psychology offers insights into
memory processes that businesses can leverage to
improve brand recognition and recall among
consumers.

One prominent concept is the primacy and
recency effects. These effects suggest that individuals

are more likely to remember information presented at the beginning (primacy) and end (recency) of a sequence (Glisky, 2011). Marketers can use this knowledge to strategically position their brand messages, ensuring that key information is presented at these memory-enhancing positions.

Additionally, research on associative networks and spreading activation provides valuable insights into how memories are interconnected (Collins & Loftus, 1975). Businesses can capitalize on this understanding by creating strong associations between their brands and positive attributes through consistent branding, emotional appeals, and memorable advertising campaigns. These associations increase the likelihood of consumers retrieving positive brand information when making purchase decisions.

Implications for Product Design and User Experience:

Understanding cognitive processes is crucial for designing user interfaces, websites, and mobile applications that enhance user experience and satisfaction. Cognitive psychology principles can inform the layout, navigation, and information organization of these interfaces.

For example, the principle of chunking suggests that breaking down information into smaller, meaningful units improves cognitive processing and reduces cognitive load (Miller, 1956). Businesses can apply this principle by organizing information into logical categories and using clear headings and subheadings. This approach helps users navigate through complex information more easily and facilitates decision-making.

Moreover, cognitive psychology emphasizes the significance of visual perception. Research indicates that consumers often rely on visual cues to form initial impressions and judgments about products and interfaces (Kardes, 2021). By applying principles of visual hierarchy, color psychology, and effective use of white space, businesses can create visually appealing interfaces that capture attention and promote positive user experiences.

Conclusion:

Cognitive psychology provides valuable insights into how consumers perceive, process, and remember information. By integrating these findings into marketing and consumer behavior strategies, businesses can design effective advertisements, product placements, and user interfaces that align with consumers' cognitive capabilities and preferences. Understanding perception, information processing, memory, and decision-making enhances the likelihood of creating favorable consumer attitudes, increasing

brand recognition and recall, and improving user

experiences. By leveraging the principles of cognitive

psychology, businesses can gain a competitive edge in

today's dynamic and information-rich market

References:

Cherry, K. (2020). Selective Attention: Definition

and Examples. Verywell Mind. Retrieved from

https://www.verywellmind.com/what-is-selective-

attention-2795022

Collins, A. M., & Loftus, E. F. (1975). A

spreading-activation theory of semantic processing.

Psychological Review, 82(6), 407-428.

Craik, F. I., & Lockhart, R. S. (1972). Levels of

processing: A framework for memory research. Journal of verbal learning and verbal behavior, 11(6), 671-684.

Glisky, E. L. (2011). Changes in cognitive function in human aging. In D. R. Riddle (Ed.), Brain Aging: Models, Methods, and Mechanisms (pp. 3-20). CRC Press/Taylor & Francis.

Kahneman, D. (2011). Thinking, fast and slow. Macmillan.

Kardes, F. R. (2021). Consumer behavior and marketing strategy. In The Handbook of Consumer Psychology and Marketing (pp. 3-27). Routledge.

Miller, G. A. (1956). The magical number seven, plus or minus two: Some limits on our capacity for processing information. Psychological Review, 63(2), 81-97.

Zajonc, R. B. (1968). Attitudinal effects of mere

exposure. Journal of Personality and Social

Psychology, 9(2), 1-27.

Chapter 4: Operant Conditioning in Human Resources: Shaping Employee Behavior for Positive Performance

In human resource management, understanding the principles of operant conditioning can be invaluable for shaping employee behavior and driving positive performance within organizations. Operant conditioning, a concept pioneered by B.F. Skinner, focuses on the relationship between behaviors and their consequences. By providing rewards or recognition for desired behaviors and implementing consequences for undesirable behaviors, organizations can effectively motivate employees and reinforce positive performance. This chapter will explore the application of operant conditioning principles in human resources, examining its benefits, strategies, and potential considerations.

<u>Benefits of Applying Operant Conditioning in Human Resources:</u>

The application of operant conditioning principles in human resources offers several benefits for organizations. Firstly, it provides a systematic approach to influence employee behavior, allowing organizations to align employee actions with desired goals and objectives. By understanding the relationship between behavior and consequences, organizations can shape behavior in a way that supports overall productivity and performance.

Secondly, operant conditioning can enhance employee motivation. By implementing a system of rewards, such as monetary incentives, recognition, or opportunities for career advancement, organizations can create a positive work environment that encourages employees to exert greater effort and achieve desired outcomes. Rewards serve as positive reinforcers, increasing the likelihood of employees repeating the desired behaviors and maintaining high levels of engagement.

<u>Strategies for Implementing Operant Conditioning in Human Resources:</u>

To effectively implement operant conditioning principles in human resources, organizations can employ various strategies tailored to their specific needs and culture. The following strategies can guide

the application of operant conditioning in shaping
employee behavior:

1. Clearly Define Desired Behaviors: The first
step is to define and communicate the desired behaviors
and performance expectations to employees. This
ensures that employees are aware of what is expected of
them and what behaviors will be reinforced.

2. Establish a Reward System: Organizations
can create a reward system that aligns with the desired
behaviors. Rewards can include monetary bonuses,
promotions, public recognition, or additional benefits.
The rewards should be meaningful and perceived as
valuable by employees to reinforce their performance.

3. Consistency in Consequences: Consistency is
essential in operant conditioning. Organizations must
ensure that consequences, both positive and negative,

are consistently applied to reinforce or discourage specific behaviors. Inconsistency can lead to confusion and diminish the effectiveness of operant conditioning techniques.

4. Continuous Feedback and Performance Evaluation: Regular feedback and performance evaluation allow organizations to provide timely reinforcement and corrective measures. Positive feedback can strengthen desired behaviors, while constructive feedback can guide employees towards improved performance.

5. Training and Development Opportunities: Providing opportunities for training and development not only enhances employee skills but also serves as a form of positive reinforcement. Offering opportunities for growth and advancement can motivate employees to exhibit desired behaviors.

Considerations and Ethical Implications:

While operant conditioning techniques can be powerful tools in shaping employee behavior, it is crucial to consider ethical implications and potential challenges. Organizations should be mindful of the following considerations:

1. Avoiding Manipulation: Employers must strike a balance between using operant conditioning techniques to shape behavior and avoiding manipulative practices. It is important to respect employees' autonomy and not employ excessive control or coercion.

2. Individual Differences: Employees may respond differently to reinforcement strategies due to their unique personalities, backgrounds, and motivations. Organizations should consider individual

differences and tailor their approaches to ensure fairness and inclusivity.

3. Over-reliance on Extrinsic Motivation: While rewards can motivate employees, over-reliance on extrinsic motivation may diminish intrinsic motivation. Organizations should foster a work environment that also emphasizes intrinsic rewards, such as meaningful work, autonomy, and opportunities for self-expression.

4. Long-Term Sustainability: Organizations should evaluate the long-term sustainability of their reward systems. Constantly increasing rewards without corresponding improvements in performance may lead to diminishing returns and undermine the effectiveness of operant conditioning techniques.

Conclusion:

Operant conditioning principles provide valuable insights for human resource management, enabling organizations to shape employee behavior and drive positive performance. By utilizing rewards and consequences, organizations can create an environment that motivates employees and aligns their actions with organizational goals. However, it is essential to implement operant conditioning strategies ethically, considering individual differences and long-term sustainability. By doing so, organizations can maximize the potential benefits of operant conditioning in human resources and create a positive and productive workplace.

Resources:

Skinner, B. F. (1953). Science and Human Behavior.

Free Press.

Milkovich, G. T., Newman, J. M., & Gerhart, B.

(2021). Compensation (13th ed.). McGraw-Hill

Education.

Latham, G. P., & Pinder, C. C. (2005). Work

motivation theory and research at the dawn of the

twenty-first century. Annual Review of Psychology,

56, 485-516.

Deci, E. L., & Ryan, R. M. (1985). Intrinsic

motivation and self-determination in human

behavior. Springer.

Chapter 5: Social Psychology in Business: Enhancing Customer Relations, Networking, and Partnerships

In today's competitive business landscape, organizations strive to establish strong connections with customers, foster effective networking practices, and form mutually beneficial partnerships. Social psychology, a branch of psychology that focuses on understanding how individuals' thoughts, feelings, and behaviors are influenced by others, offers valuable insights and strategies to achieve these goals. This chapter explores the application of social psychology concepts in customer relations, networking, and partnerships within the business context.

<u>Understanding Social Influence:</u>

Social influence refers to the impact that others have on an individual's attitudes, beliefs, and behaviors. In the realm of customer relations, businesses can leverage social influence to build rapport and enhance customer satisfaction. For example, utilizing social proof by displaying positive customer reviews or testimonials can influence potential customers to trust the brand and make a purchase (Cialdini, 2009). Additionally, understanding the principles of conformity can help businesses tailor their marketing efforts to align with social norms and trends, thereby increasing the appeal of their products or services (Asch, 1955).

Group Dynamics and Teamwork:

Group dynamics play a crucial role in both internal and external business interactions. Within organizations, social psychology principles can inform team dynamics and collaboration, ultimately leading to improved productivity and innovation. Research suggests that cohesive teams with shared goals tend to outperform those with weak group dynamics (Hackman & Morris, 2009). By fostering a positive team climate, encouraging effective communication, and promoting shared decision-making, businesses can harness the power of group dynamics to drive success.

In the context of customer relations, understanding group dynamics can help businesses tap into the influence of reference groups on consumer behavior. Reference groups are social groups that individuals use as a basis for comparison, identification, and decision-making. By identifying relevant reference groups for their target customers, businesses can tailor marketing strategies that resonate with the values, aspirations, and preferences of those groups (Bearden & Etzel, 1982). This approach can enhance customer loyalty and attract new customers through word-of-mouth referrals.

<u>Interpersonal Relationships and Customer Satisfaction:</u>

Building strong interpersonal relationships with customers is vital for fostering loyalty and satisfaction. Social psychology research emphasizes the significance of empathy, trust, and communication in forming and maintaining relationships. By demonstrating empathy and active listening skills, businesses can understand customer needs, address concerns, and provide personalized experiences (Davis & Oathout, 1987). Furthermore, establishing trust through consistent and transparent interactions can enhance customer satisfaction and loyalty (Mayer, Davis, & Schoorman, 1995).

Networking: Expanding Connections and Opportunities:

Networking is a crucial aspect of professional success, enabling individuals and businesses to forge connections, exchange information, and create new opportunities. Social psychology principles offer valuable insights into effective networking strategies. One such principle is the reciprocity norm, which suggests that individuals feel obliged to return favors or acts of kindness (Gouldner, 1960). Applying this principle in networking situations, businesses can initiate positive interactions, provide value to others, and foster mutually beneficial relationships.

Additionally, understanding the social exchange theory can guide networking practices. This theory posits that individuals engage in social interactions with the expectation of receiving rewards or benefits in return (Homans, 1958). By recognizing the needs and interests of networking partners and offering meaningful contributions, businesses can establish strong networks and leverage them for professional growth, referrals, and collaborations.

<u>Partnerships: Building Mutually Beneficial Relationships:</u>

Forming partnerships is a strategic approach for businesses to enhance their capabilities, access new markets, and achieve shared objectives. Social psychology concepts can inform the development and maintenance of successful partnerships. One relevant concept is the principle of perceived fairness and equity, which suggests that individuals seek fairness in relationships and exchanges (Adams, 1965). Applying this principle, businesses can ensure that partnerships are built on equitable terms, where both parties perceive the benefits and contributions to be balanced.

Another crucial concept is interdependence theory, which highlights the importance of mutual goals and shared rewards in fostering strong partnerships (Kelley & Thibaut, 1978). By aligning objectives, clearly defining roles and responsibilities, and establishing open lines of communication, businesses can nurture partnerships that thrive on cooperation, trust, and mutual benefit.

Conclusion:

Incorporating social psychology principles into customer relations, networking, and partnerships can significantly enhance business outcomes. By understanding social influence, group dynamics, and interpersonal relationships, businesses can build rapport with customers, develop strong networks, and establish mutually beneficial partnerships. Employing strategies rooted in social psychology research can lead to increased customer satisfaction, improved networking practices, and fruitful collaborative ventures, ultimately contributing to long-term success in today's dynamic business environment.

References:

Adams, J. S. (1965). Inequity in social exchange.

Advances in Experimental Social Psychology, 2, 267-299.

Asch, S. E. (1955). Opinions and social pressure.

Scientific American, 193(5), 31-35.

Bearden, W. O., & Etzel, M. J. (1982). Reference

group influence on product and brand purchase

decisions. Journal of Consumer Research, 9(2), 183-

194.

Cialdini, R. B. (2009). Influence: Science and

practice (5th ed.). Pearson.

Davis, M. H., & Oathout, H. A. (1987).

Maintenance of satisfaction in romantic

relationships: Empathy and relational competence.

Journal of Personality and Social Psychology, 53(2),

397-410.

Gouldner, A. W. (1960). The norm of reciprocity: A

preliminary statement. American Sociological

Review, 25(2), 161-178.

Hackman, J. R., & Morris, C. G. (2009). Group

dynamics: An introduction. In J. L. Nye & A. M.

Brower (Eds.), What's social about social

cognition? Research on socially shared cognition in

small groups (pp. 3-30). American Psychological

Association.

Homans, G. C. (1958). Social behavior as exchange.

American Journal of Sociology, 63(6), 597-606.

Kelley, H. H., & Thibaut, J. W. (1978).

Interpersonal relations: A theory of interdependence.

Wiley.

Mayer, R. C., Davis, J. H., & Schoorman, F. D.

(1995). An integrative model of organizational trust.

Academy of Management Review, 20(3), 709-734.

Chapter 6: Developmental Psychology and its Application in Human Resource Practices

Developmental psychology is a branch of psychology that focuses on the study of human growth and development across the lifespan. It examines the physical, cognitive, emotional, and social changes individuals undergo as they progress from infancy to old age. The knowledge and insights derived from developmental psychology can be instrumental in informing human resource practices within organizations. By recognizing the unique needs and abilities of employees at different stages of their careers, businesses can design more effective training programs, implement targeted performance management strategies, and foster meaningful career development opportunities. This chapter explores the application of developmental psychology in human resource practices, highlighting the benefits and implications for organizational success.

Understanding Developmental Stages and Milestones:

Developmental psychology identifies key stages and milestones that individuals typically experience throughout their lives. These stages, such as infancy, childhood, adolescence, adulthood, and old age, are characterized by distinct physical, cognitive, and socio-emotional changes. By understanding these developmental stages and milestones, organizations can tailor their human resource practices to meet the specific needs and requirements of employees at each stage.

<u>Infancy and Early Childhood:</u>

During infancy and early childhood, individuals experience rapid physical and cognitive development. Human resource practices can recognize the importance of providing a supportive and nurturing work environment for employees who are parents or caregivers of young children. Offering flexible work arrangements, parental leave policies, and on-site childcare facilities can contribute to employee satisfaction, retention, and work-life balance (Johnson & Johnson, 2021). Moreover, training programs and performance management strategies for this group should consider their cognitive abilities and learning styles, ensuring information is presented in a clear and concise manner.

<u>Adolescence:</u>

Adolescence is a period characterized by significant physical, cognitive, and socio-emotional changes. Human resource practices can adapt to the unique needs of adolescent employees by providing mentorship programs, internships, and skill-building opportunities. Recognizing their desire for independence, autonomy, and self-expression, organizations can foster an environment that encourages creative thinking, decision-making, and personal growth (Steinberg & Morris, 2001).

<u>Adulthood:</u>

Adulthood spans several stages, including early, middle, and late adulthood. Human resource practices can recognize the diverse needs and priorities of employees during these stages. In early adulthood, organizations can offer professional development programs, career counseling, and opportunities for skill acquisition to facilitate career advancement. During midlife, employees may seek work-life balance and the opportunity to contribute meaningfully. Flexible work arrangements, sabbatical programs, and wellness initiatives can help support employees' overall well-being and job satisfaction. In late adulthood, organizations can provide phased retirement options, mentoring opportunities, and recognition programs to acknowledge the experience and wisdom of older employees (Bal, De Lange, Jansen, & Van der Velde, 2011).

<u>Effective Training Programs:</u>

Applying developmental psychology in training programs can optimize learning outcomes and skill development. Tailoring training methods to the specific cognitive abilities, learning styles, and experience levels of employees can enhance their engagement and knowledge retention. For example, utilizing interactive and hands-on training approaches, incorporating real-life examples, and providing opportunities for practice and feedback can improve skill acquisition (Hodgkinson & Sparrow, 2002). Furthermore, considering the developmental stage of employees, training programs can be designed to align with their career aspirations and growth potential.

<u>Performance Management Strategies:</u>

Performance management encompasses processes such as goal setting, feedback, performance appraisal, and career development. Developmental psychology insights can guide the implementation of effective performance management strategies. By considering employees' developmental stages and career goals, organizations can set realistic and meaningful performance objectives. Providing regular feedback and coaching tailored to employees' specific

needs and abilities can support their professional

growth and performance improvement (Murphy &

Cleveland, 1995). Moreover, recognizing the

importance of ongoing skill development, organizations

can offer opportunities for training, stretch assignments,

and cross-functional experiences to nurture employees'

potential.

Career Development Opportunities:

Applying developmental psychology principles

in career development can benefit both employees and

organizations. Recognizing employees' developmental

stages and career aspirations, organizations can provide

personalized career planning, succession planning, and

mentoring programs. These initiatives can help

employees navigate their career paths, identify growth

opportunities, and acquire the necessary skills and

competencies (Arnold & Cohen, 2008). Offering diverse job assignments, rotational programs, and promotions based on merit can motivate employees and foster loyalty and retention.

Implications and Benefits for Organizational Success:

The application of developmental psychology in human resource practices offers several benefits for organizational success. By aligning training programs, performance management strategies, and career development opportunities with employees' developmental needs, organizations can enhance employee engagement, job satisfaction, and productivity (Saks & Gruman, 2014). A well-designed and tailored approach to human resource practices can also attract top talent, promote employee retention, and create a positive organizational culture that values growth and development (Werner & DeSimone, 2012).

<u>Conclusion:</u>

Developmental psychology provides valuable insights into human growth and development across the lifespan. By applying these principles to human resource practices, organizations can optimize their training programs, performance management strategies, and career development opportunities. Recognizing the unique needs and abilities of employees at different stages of their careers contributes to more effective talent management, employee satisfaction, and organizational success. By embracing the principles of developmental psychology, organizations can foster a supportive work environment that nurtures individual growth, maximizes potential, and encourages lifelong learning.

References:

Arnold, J., & Cohen, L. (2008). Psychology and work: Perspectives on industrial and organizational psychology. Psychology Press.

Bal, P. M., De Lange, A. H., Jansen, P. G., & Van der Velde, M. (2011). Age and trust as moderators in the relation between procedural justice and turnover: A large-scale longitudinal study. Applied Psychology, 60(3), 336-355.

Hodgkinson, G. P., & Sparrow, P. R. (2002). The competence of managers: A review, critique, and future research agenda. Journal of Management, 28(2), 151-178.

Johnson & Johnson. (2021). Supporting Working Parents. Retrieved from https://www.jnj.com/caring/supported-working-parents

Murphy, K. R., & Cleveland, J. N. (1995).

Understanding performance appraisal: Social,

organizational, and goal-based perspectives. SAGE

Publications.

Saks, A. M., & Gruman, J. A. (2014). What do we

really know about employee engagement? Human

Resource Development Quarterly, 25(2), 155-182.

Steinberg, L., & Morris, A. S. (2001). Adolescent

development. Annual Review of Psychology, 52(1),

83-110.

Werner, J. M., & DeSimone, R. L. (2012). Human

resource development (6th ed.). South-Western

Cengage Learning.

Chapter 7: Abnormal Psychology in the Workplace: Managing Employee Well-being and Mental Health

Abnormal psychology refers to the study of atypical patterns of behavior, emotions, and cognition that deviate from the societal norms. In the context of the workplace, knowledge of abnormal psychology can be instrumental in managing employee well-being and mental health. This chapter explores the significance of understanding abnormal psychology in the workplace, highlighting the benefits of promoting a supportive and inclusive work environment, providing resources for mental health support, and reducing stigma surrounding mental health. By implementing strategies informed by abnormal psychology, organizations can positively impact employee morale and productivity.

Importance of Abnormal Psychology in the Workplace:

Abnormal psychology plays a crucial role in creating a workplace culture that prioritizes employee well-being and mental health. Employees facing mental health challenges may experience reduced productivity, increased absenteeism, and poor job satisfaction, leading to negative outcomes for both individuals and organizations. By recognizing the signs of mental health issues and implementing appropriate interventions, employers can foster a healthier work environment and support their employees effectively.

Promoting a Supportive and Inclusive Work Environment:

Creating a supportive and inclusive work environment is fundamental to the well-being of employees. When individuals feel valued, respected, and supported, they are more likely to seek help for mental health concerns and actively engage in their work. Strategies for promoting a supportive work environment include:

1. Encouraging open communication: Establishing channels for employees to express their concerns, whether through regular team meetings, suggestion boxes, or confidential reporting systems, fosters a culture of openness and encourages dialogue about mental health.

2. Providing mental health training: Offering training programs to increase awareness and understanding of mental health issues can equip

managers and employees with the knowledge and skills to recognize and respond to signs of distress effectively.

3. Offering flexible work arrangements: Implementing flexible work options, such as remote work, flexible hours, or job sharing, can help employees manage their mental health and achieve a better work-life balance.

4. Cultivating a positive work culture: Encouraging teamwork, recognizing achievements, and promoting a positive work environment through team-building activities and appreciation initiatives can contribute to employees' psychological well-being.

Providing Resources for Mental Health Support:

Organizations can support employees' mental health by providing resources and access to appropriate

mental health support services. Some effective
strategies include:

1. Employee assistance programs (EAPs):
Implementing EAPs can provide employees with
confidential access to professional counselors who can
help address personal and work-related concerns,
including mental health issues.

2. Mental health benefits and insurance
coverage: Ensuring that mental health services are
included in employee benefits packages and that
insurance coverage adequately supports mental health
treatment can remove barriers to seeking help.

3. Access to mental health professionals:
Collaborating with mental health professionals, such as
psychologists or therapists, and offering onsite
counseling or facilitating referrals to external providers,

can enhance employees' access to mental health support.

4. Peer support programs: Establishing peer support networks or employee resource groups focused on mental health can provide a safe space for individuals to connect, share experiences, and provide support to one another.

Reducing Stigma Surrounding Mental Health:

Addressing the stigma associated with mental health is crucial for creating an environment where employees feel comfortable seeking help without fear of judgment or negative consequences. Strategies for reducing stigma include:

1. Education and awareness campaigns: Organizing workshops, seminars, or lunch-and-learn sessions to educate employees about common mental

health conditions, their impact, and available resources can help dispel misconceptions and reduce stigma.

2. Leadership commitment: Encouraging leaders and managers to openly discuss mental health, share personal experiences, and demonstrate support for employees seeking help can send a powerful message that mental health matters and is a priority in the organization.

3. Language and communication: Promoting the use of inclusive and non-stigmatizing language in all communications, policies, and procedures can contribute to a culture of acceptance and understanding.

4. Celebrating diverse experiences: Recognizing and celebrating the diverse experiences and strengths of employees, including those who have overcome mental

health challenges, can help reduce stigma and foster a more inclusive work environment.

Conclusion:

Abnormal psychology provides valuable insights into managing employee well-being and mental health in the workplace. By promoting a supportive and inclusive work environment, providing resources for mental health support, and reducing stigma surrounding mental health, organizations can positively impact employee morale and productivity. Recognizing the importance of abnormal psychology in the workplace not only supports individual employees but also contributes to a healthier, more engaged workforce and a more successful organization.

References:

Nieuwenhuijsen, K., Faber, B., Verbeek, J. H.,

Neumeyer-Gromen, A., Hees, H. L., Verhoeven, A.

C., ... & van der Feltz-Cornelis, C. M. (2014).

Interventions to improve return to work in depressed

people. Cochrane Database of Systematic Reviews,

(12).

Pranjic, N., Males-Bilic, L., & Beganlic, A. (2020).

Employee Assistance Programs and Workplace

Counselling: Promoting Employee Mental Health

and Well-Being. International Journal of

Environmental Research and Public Health, 17(17),

6255.

World Health Organization. (2019). Mental health

in the workplace. Retrieved from

https://www.who.int/mental_health/in_the_workplac

e/en/

Mental Health Commission of Canada. (2017).

Making the case for investing in mental health in

Canada. Retrieved from

https://www.mentalhealthcommission.ca/sites/defaul

t/files/2017-

03/Investing_in_Mental_Health_FINAL_Version_E

NG.pdf

Chapter 8: Biological Psychology and its Implications for Operations and Marketing

Biological psychology, also known as biopsychology or psychobiology, explores the intricate relationship between biological processes and human behavior. Understanding the impact of biological factors on behavior can provide valuable insights for businesses, particularly in operations and marketing. This chapter will delve into the ways in which biological psychology can inform and shape business practices. Specifically, it will focus on how studying consumer responses to sensory stimuli, such as colors, scents, and music, can help businesses create environments that enhance

customer experiences and influence purchasing
decisions.

<u>Biological Psychology and Consumer Behavior:</u>

Biological psychology recognizes that our sensory systems play a crucial role in shaping our behavior and decision-making processes. By studying consumer responses to sensory stimuli, businesses can gain a deeper understanding of how these stimuli impact customer experiences, preferences, and purchasing decisions.

Colors: Color psychology suggests that different colors evoke distinct emotional and psychological responses in individuals. For instance, warm colors like red and orange can stimulate excitement and urgency, making them suitable for sales and promotional materials. On the other hand, cool colors like blue and green are often associated with calmness and relaxation, which can be beneficial in settings where customers seek a serene atmosphere. Understanding the impact of colors on consumer behavior can guide businesses in creating visually appealing marketing materials, store layouts, and product packaging that align with their target audience's emotional and cognitive responses (Hansen, 2019).

Scents: Research has shown that scents can evoke powerful emotional and cognitive associations, which can significantly impact consumer behavior. Pleasant aromas have been linked to positive emotional states and enhanced customer experiences. For example, the use of fragrances in retail environments has been found to increase customers' willingness to spend more time in stores and positively influence their evaluations of products. Moreover, specific scents, such as lavender or citrus, have been associated with relaxation or invigoration, respectively, and can be strategically employed to enhance customers' mood and overall shopping experience (Spangenberg et al., 2015).

Music: The influence of music on consumer behavior has been widely studied in the field of psychology. Background music in stores and restaurants can affect customers' emotional states, perceptions of waiting time, and willingness to make purchases. Faster tempo music tends to increase arousal and can be suitable for environments where quick decision-making is desired, such as fast-food restaurants. In contrast, slower tempo music can create a relaxed atmosphere and promote a leisurely shopping experience. The genre of music also matters, as different genres evoke unique emotional responses. By carefully selecting the right music, businesses can shape customer experiences and create a favorable ambiance that supports their marketing objectives (North et al., 2020).

<u>Implications for Operations:</u>

Understanding the impact of biological factors on behavior can also have practical implications for operational decisions within a business.

Store Layout and Design: By incorporating knowledge from biological psychology, businesses can optimize their store layout and design to improve customer experiences. For example, understanding that certain colors promote specific emotional responses can guide the choice of color schemes for different sections of the store. Likewise, considering the impact of scents on customers' moods and behaviors can inform decisions regarding the use of ambient fragrances in specific areas of the store. Moreover, understanding the influence of music on customers' arousal levels and perceived waiting time can help in selecting appropriate playlists and sound systems for different areas of the store (Dobni et al., 2018).

Product Placement and Packaging: Biological psychology insights can also be applied to product placement and packaging. For instance, understanding the impact of colors on consumer behavior can guide the selection of packaging colors that elicit the desired emotional responses or convey specific brand messages. Additionally, considering the influence of scents on consumer perceptions can inform decisions about using scent-infused packaging or incorporating scratch-and-sniff features to enhance the sensory appeal of products (Lemke et al., 2017).

Implications for Marketing:

Biological psychology findings can significantly inform marketing strategies and tactics, enabling businesses to connect with their target audience more effectively.

Advertising and Branding: Incorporating knowledge about color psychology into advertising and branding efforts can help businesses evoke desired emotional responses in consumers. The careful use of color in advertisements, websites, and promotional materials can create a visual appeal that resonates with the target audience and enhances brand recognition. Similarly, understanding the influence of scents on consumer behavior can be leveraged in marketing campaigns to evoke specific associations and create memorable brand experiences (Labrecque et al., 2013).

E-commerce and Online Experiences: The principles of biological psychology are also relevant in the context of e-commerce and online experiences. The use of appropriate colors, appealing visuals, and engaging auditory elements can enhance the online shopping experience. Businesses can optimize website design, user interfaces, and multimedia elements to create a sensory-rich online environment that aligns with the preferences and expectations of their target customers (Huang et al., 2020).

<u>Conclusion:</u>

Biological psychology provides valuable insights into the impact of biological factors on behavior, and this knowledge can be effectively applied in operations and marketing. By understanding consumer responses to sensory stimuli such as colors, scents, and music, businesses can create environments and experiences that enhance customer satisfaction, influence purchasing decisions, and strengthen brand loyalty. Incorporating these insights into store layouts, product packaging, advertising campaigns, and online experiences allows businesses to create a sensory-rich environment that resonates with their target audience, ultimately leading to improved business performance.

References:

Dobni, C. B., Ritchie, R. J. B., & Zerbe, W. J.

(2018). Retail atmospherics: The impact of the sensory environment on consumers. Journal of Business Research, 86, 373-381.

Hansen, T. L. (2019). Color and psychological functioning: A review of theoretical and empirical work. Frontiers in Psychology, 10, 2766.

Huang, C. Y., Zhang, K. Z., & Pleshko, L. (2020).

The interactive effect of sensory information cues and website interactivity on online consumer behavior. Journal of Interactive Marketing, 51, 1-14.

Labrecque, L. I., Patrick, V. M., Milne, G. R., & Deighton, J. (2013). The marketers' prismatic palette: A review of color research and future directions. Psychology & Marketing, 30(2), 187-202.

Lemke, M. R., Mattsson, B., & Siegrist, M. (2017). Do the colors of food packaging affect taste and flavor perception in humans? Foods, 6(5), 34.

North, A. C., Hargreaves, D. J., & McKendrick, J. (2020). The effects of music tempo and loudness level on treadmill exercise. Psychology of Sport and Exercise, 47, 101588.

Spangenberg, E. R., Crowley, A. E., & Henderson,

P. W. (2015). Improving the store environment: Do

olfactory cues affect evaluations and behaviors?

Journal of Marketing, 79(2), 21-37.

Chapter 9: Psychodynamic Theory in Human Resources and Leadership: Unconscious Motives, Personal History, and Interpersonal Dynamics

Psychodynamic theory, developed by Sigmund Freud, explores the interplay between conscious and unconscious mental processes, emphasizing the role of unconscious motives, personal history, and interpersonal dynamics in shaping human behavior. While traditionally associated with psychoanalysis and therapy, psychodynamic principles have relevance beyond the clinical setting. This chapter will discuss how psychodynamic theory can inform practices in human resources (HR) and leadership, highlighting its applications in effective leadership styles, team building, and conflict resolution strategies. By recognizing and understanding the underlying psychological factors at play, organizations can foster a healthier work environment, enhance employee engagement, and promote successful leadership.

Understanding Unconscious Motives:

Psychodynamic theory asserts that unconscious motives, which are outside an individual's conscious awareness, influence thoughts, emotions, and behaviors. In the context of HR and leadership, recognizing and understanding these unconscious motives can be instrumental in understanding employee behavior and motivations. Employees' unconscious desires for recognition, achievement, or power may drive their actions, affecting their job performance and engagement levels.

<u>Leadership Styles:</u>

Psychodynamic theory suggests that leadership styles can be influenced by unconscious motives and unresolved conflicts from personal history. For instance, a leader who experienced a lack of recognition or authority during their formative years may strive for dominance and control in their leadership role. By being aware of these unconscious motives, leaders can reflect on their own behaviors and adjust their leadership styles accordingly. They can focus on creating a supportive environment that fosters trust, encourages open communication, and provides opportunities for growth and recognition.

<u>Team Building:</u>

Psychodynamic principles also play a role in team dynamics and collaboration. Each team member brings their own unique personal history and unconscious motivations to the group. Understanding these factors can help leaders build effective teams by considering individuals' strengths, weaknesses, and personality traits. By recognizing and addressing potential conflicts or unresolved issues within the team, leaders can promote a healthier and more cohesive work environment.

Conflict Resolution Strategies:

Conflict is an inevitable aspect of workplace interactions, and psychodynamic theory provides insights into understanding and resolving conflicts effectively. Conflict often arises from unconscious motives, past experiences, and underlying tensions among individuals. HR professionals and leaders can apply psychodynamic principles to create a safe space for open dialogue, encourage active listening, and facilitate conflict resolution processes that address the root causes of conflict rather than surface-level disagreements. By identifying and acknowledging the unconscious dynamics at play, leaders can help employees work through conflicts and find mutually satisfactory solutions.

Conclusion:

Psychodynamic theory offers valuable insights into the unconscious motives, personal history, and interpersonal dynamics that influence human behavior. By applying these principles in HR and leadership practices, organizations can foster effective leadership styles, build strong teams, and implement successful conflict resolution strategies. Recognizing the impact of unconscious processes allows leaders to create a supportive work environment, promote employee engagement, and develop a culture of open communication. By integrating psychodynamic principles into their approach, HR professionals and leaders can enhance employee satisfaction, improve teamwork, and drive organizational success.

Resources:

Freud, S. (1915). The unconscious. Standard Edition, 14, 159-214.

Hogan, R., & Kaiser, R. B. (2005). What we know about leadership. Review of General Psychology, 9(2), 169-180.

Jung, C. G. (1968). The structure and dynamics of the psyche. Collected Works of C. G. Jung, Vol. 8.

Obholzer, A., & Roberts, V. Z. (1994). The unconscious at work: Individual and organizational stress in the human services. Routledge.

Stevens, A., & Price, J. (1996). Evolutionary

psychiatry: A new beginning. Routledge.

Chapter 10: Positive Psychology in Business: Enhancing Employee Satisfaction, Customer Loyalty, and Well-being

Positive psychology, a branch of psychology focused on studying human strengths, well-being, and flourishing, offers valuable insights and strategies that can be applied to various aspects of business operations. By incorporating positive psychology principles into customer relations and human resource practices, organizations can foster a positive work culture, leverage employee strengths, and promote work-life balance, ultimately leading to higher employee engagement, customer satisfaction, and overall well-being. This chapter explores the significance of positive psychology in the business context, highlighting its potential benefits and providing practical recommendations for its implementation.

<u>Positive Psychology in Customer Relations:</u>

Incorporating positive psychology principles in customer relations is essential for creating positive customer experiences, building customer loyalty, and generating customer satisfaction. Research has shown that positive emotions can enhance customers' perceptions of service quality and increase their likelihood of repeat purchases (Fredrickson, 2003). By focusing on positive emotions, businesses can design customer interactions that foster positive experiences, such as training customer service representatives to be empathetic, attentive, and responsive to customer needs

(Cohn & Fredrickson, 2010). Implementing positive psychology interventions in customer relations can lead to improved customer satisfaction, increased customer loyalty, and positive word-of-mouth recommendations.

Moreover, the concept of strengths-based approach, derived from positive psychology, can be applied in customer relations. Recognizing and leveraging customers' strengths, such as their unique preferences or skills, can enhance their satisfaction and engagement with a product or service. For instance, businesses can personalize their offerings based on customers' strengths and provide tailored recommendations, resulting in a more meaningful and positive customer experience (Linley, Willars, & Biswas-Diener, 2010).

Positive Psychology in Human Resource Practices:

Positive psychology principles are equally relevant in human resource practices, influencing employee satisfaction, engagement, and overall well-being. Fostering a positive work culture is crucial in creating an environment that supports and nurtures employees' psychological needs. Research suggests that a positive work culture characterized by trust, respect, and gratitude can lead to higher job satisfaction, reduced turnover, and increased employee commitment (Cameron, Bright, & Caza, 2004).

Emphasizing employee strengths is another important aspect of positive psychology in human resource practices. By recognizing and utilizing employees' strengths, organizations can enhance their job satisfaction and performance. This can be achieved by providing training and development opportunities that align with employees' strengths, assigning tasks that allow them to utilize their strengths, and offering feedback and recognition for their contributions (Luthans, Avey, Avolio, Norman, & Combs, 2006). Leveraging employee strengths not only boosts individual well-being but also contributes to overall team productivity and organizational success.

Promoting work-life balance is another critical component of positive psychology in human resource practices. Balancing work and personal life is crucial for employees' well-being, satisfaction, and productivity. Organizations can facilitate work-life balance by implementing flexible work arrangements, promoting employee autonomy and control over their work schedules, and encouraging employees to prioritize self-care and maintain healthy boundaries (Greenhaus & Powell, 2006). Such practices contribute to reduced stress levels, increased job satisfaction, and improved overall well-being.

<u>Implementation Strategies:</u>

Implementing positive psychology principles requires a systematic approach that involves integrating them into various aspects of the organization's policies, practices, and culture. Here are some practical strategies for incorporating positive psychology in customer relations and human resource practices:

1. Training and Education: Provide training programs and workshops for employees to enhance their understanding of positive psychology principles, including the importance of positive emotions, strengths-based approaches, and work-life balance.

2. Recruitment and Selection: Incorporate positive psychology principles in the recruitment and

selection process by assessing candidates' strengths, positive attitudes, and alignment with the organization's values and culture.

3. Performance Management: Develop performance management systems that focus on recognizing and reinforcing employee strengths, providing constructive feedback, and setting meaningful goals that align with employees' personal values and strengths.

4. Rewards and Recognition: Implement reward and recognition programs that acknowledge and celebrate employee achievements, emphasizing the positive impact of their contributions to the organization's success.

5. Leadership Development: Train leaders in positive leadership practices, such as fostering positive

relationships, promoting a positive work culture, and inspiring and empowering employees.

6. Employee Well-being Programs: Establish initiatives that prioritize employee well-being, such as wellness programs, stress management workshops, and work-life balance initiatives.

Conclusion:

Incorporating positive psychology principles into customer relations and human resource practices offers numerous benefits for businesses, including increased employee satisfaction, improved customer loyalty, and enhanced overall well-being. By fostering a positive work culture, leveraging employee strengths, and promoting work-life balance, organizations can create an environment that nurtures employee engagement and positively impacts customer experiences. Implementing these principles requires a systematic and holistic approach, integrating positive psychology strategies into various aspects of the organization's operations. By embracing positive psychology, businesses can create a thriving workplace and build sustainable relationships with customers, ultimately driving organizational success.

References:

Cameron, K. S., Bright, D., & Caza, A. (2004).

Exploring the relationships between organizational

virtuousness and performance. American Behavioral

Scientist, 47(6), 766-790.

Cohn, M. A., & Fredrickson, B. L. (2010). In search

of durable positive psychology interventions:

Predictors and consequences of long-term positive

behavior change. Journal of Positive Psychology,

5(5), 355-366.

Fredrickson, B. L. (2003). The value of positive

emotions: The emerging science of positive

psychology is coming to understand why it's good to

feel good. American Scientist, 91(4), 330-335.

Greenhaus, J. H., & Powell, G. N. (2006). When

work and family are allies: A theory of work-family enrichment. Academy of Management Review, 31(1), 72-92.

Linley, P. A., Willars, J., & Biswas-Diener, R. (Eds.). (2010). The strengths book: Be confident, be successful, and enjoy better relationships by realizing the best of you. CAPP Press.

Luthans, F., Avey, J. B., Avolio, B. J., Norman, S. M., & Combs, G. M. (2006). Psychological capital development: Toward a micro-intervention. Journal of Organizational Behavior, 27(3), 387-393.